Observations

of a

Guidance

Counselor

by

Marcia

Horenstein

With Love to Sidney

CONTENTS

Opening Observation

Whenever someone says the words "guidance counselor," you know 99.9 % o f the time some negative remark will follow. Ask a student, "What was your guidance counselor like?" "Oh, I hardly ever saw her." "Her office was always too crowded. I couldn't wait." "She was never there." "She didn't even know my name."

Ask a parent about their child's guidance counselor and they will tell you how she couldn't tell them what field to go in to when they were in high school. Or recount how a white guidance counselor told them not to become a "doctor" – "lawyer" – "go to a good college" – because they weren't qualified – that they were told to do something lesser. And, as it turns out, they were perfectly capable of achieving their goals.

Teachers think guidance counselors have a cushy job with access to a telephone and "what do they do really?" They also say that guidance counselors take the students side against them.

And the school administration, if they have any paperwork task and can't decide who ought to do it, they say "the guidance counselors can do it."

And what about the Department of Education, the Mayor and the Chancellor? The last time any chancellor had anything very nice to say about counselors was Joe Fernandez, who on at least two occasions told how much his counselor helped him when he was in high school and what an important TURNING POINT it was in his life.

I can see the negative attitude toward guidance counselors reflected in two recent comments -- one by our first lady Michelle Obama who said counselors were among the school faculty that discouraged her when she was in school. "While Mrs. Obama's parents pushed her to achieve, she says teachers, counselors and classmates often questioned her abilities and potential." This appeared in an article in The New York Times on Saturday, May 16, 2009.

Second by then Labor Secretary Hilda L. Solis, appointed

by Barack Obama. Hilda Solis often recalls some advice

her high school guidance counselor gave her mother: 'Your

daughter is not college material. Maybe she should follow

the career of her older sister and become a secretary.' This

was in the opening paragraph of an article printed in The

New York Times on Monday, July 6th, 2009. Hilda Solis

was the first Latina ever to be appointed to the Cabinet and

was a four term congresswoman before that.

And now, what about College Admissions

departments, NYU for example and most other private

colleges ask for a guidance counselors recommendation

with instructions such as:

"Please describe the applicant's academic

and personal characteristics. We are particularly interested

in evidence about the candidate's intellectual prowess,

motivation and relative maturity, integrity, independence,

originality, initiative, leadership potential, capacity for growth, special talents and enthusiasm ."

The College Admissions Officers take it for granted that the counselor knows the seniors in their caseload very well and can discuss their students in a way that is forthright and interesting and personal.

And the press – most of the time a counselor is depicted as a harried individual frenetically going from one task to the next with not enough time, really, for any one student. The next depiction is negative, with the guidance counselor participating in something negative.

And finally, Assistant Principals (APs) who are the heads of guidance look at counselors this way: They do not have time to do the job they were prepared for in graduate school, namely counseling. There is no time for that in the opinion of Assistant Principals of guidance. So what are they doing, then?

One of the APs of Guidance that I worked under didn't want to be considered a guidance counselor. She appeared to think of it as negative based on her own experience – a white, prejudiced bitch who undervalued her. One of the Principals I worked under had the same experience. Her guidance counselor, she told us, told her not to go to college.

There is a feeling that white counselors are prejudiced – a deep rooted, long felt insulted feeling of potential thwarted by white counselors.

EXAMPLES OF WHAT THE FAMILIES OF HIGH SCHOOLERS EXPECT FROM THEIR SON OR DAUGHTER'S GUIDANCE COUNSELOR

"YOU are the guidance counselor! How come nobody called me. My niece has 45 cuts!" This was the expectation of the aunt of one of our students during a transfer conference. Her niece, who lives with her, was suspended for being involved in a gang-related incident that almost caused a riot. Her parent was asked to attend an important meeting with the AP of Guidance but did not show up.

When the counselor asked, both the student's aunt and her father, who was also present, said they had not attended parent conferences in the Fall term, at which time they would, of course, have received a clear assessment of their child's performance seven weeks into the term.

Yet when the aunt said . "YOU are the guidance counselor. How come nobody called me.?" It sounded logical. The AP of Security who was facilitating the meeting didn't rush in and say, "the teachers are supposed to call the parents because they are the ones who actually see that a child has been cutting or absent on a daily basis." The guidance counselor had to say that but alone without the comraderly support of the AP and Dean, who was also attending the meeting. And yes, as staff members know, our Principal -- at the time -- adamantly believed that the classroom teacher ought to make such calls since it is they who see when students are absent and know immediately when they fail their tests.   Yet it puts counselors in a negative light because the expectations of parents are that the guidance counselor will call.

WHAT STUDENTS EXPECT FROM THEIR GUIDANCE COUNSELOR

Students believe that a counselor should be able to give them a copy of their transcript, an extra copy of their programs and an extra copy of their report cards whenever they ask for these items . The main flaw in the work of a guidance counselor is that what students and parents want is time. They want a satisfactory amount of time with the counselor whenever they need it --when they call, when they drop in to school. Students want attention immediately for whatever question they have or whatever request they have to make and they want it NOW.

When you read how satisfactory college counselors are, how they are praised -- I'm talking about the ones parents pay good money to work with their sons and daughters -- the performance is more often than not unfavorably compared to the perfunctory encounter with the school counselor who, they say, could not offer any advice or know-how. Students and parents want to talk to a counselor in private, in a welcoming office. Nothing else is satisfactory.

WHAT GUIDANCE COUNSELORS EXPECT OF THEMSELVES

There is a great feeling of not performing up to expectations by the guidance counselors themselves because every time they are engaged in paperwork or programming, they are not doing what their master's degree focused on -- Counseling and getting to know each student very well so that the students have a sense of belonging regardless of other relationships in their lives that may be negative.

Graduate school preparation to be a guidance counselor focuses on group work and on interviewing techniques as well as how people learn (psychology). The idea is to be non critical and as Carl Rogers, the psychologist, espouses demonstrate unconditional, positive regard toward your students.

Much practice is given in this area in graduate school. Counselors are very familiar with the psychological techniques – which is how the mind learns. For example, you can learn behavior by watching someone else (modeling); you can learn behavior by trial and error. By being as genuine as possible, the counselor is a role model to the students they interact with.

Counselors are also well versed in statistics at the graduate level so that they can easily use data -- and do -- to deepen a student's vision of improvements needed academically.

"UNCONDITIONAL POSITIVE REGARD"

"Unconditional Positive Regard." That is Carl Rogers philosophy in dealing with people in a therapeutic situation. It also requires a genuineness on the part of the counselor. It is this that distinguishes a guidance counselor's method of interacting with students from a parent, teacher or dean. A bond of trust is supposed to develop between counselor and students.

An example of unconditional positive regard would be putting aside whatever you are doing every time a student comes to see you and giving them your immediate attention. If a counselor is swamped with paperwork or talking to another person, the model counselor would not say "I'm busy" or "later" or "I can't see you now" in a harried voice.

A guidance counselor would stop their paperwork to acknowledge the student's presence, say hello, and ask the student what is on their mind. The same time it takes to say something negative can be used to ask the student what it is that brought them to my office. Most of the time the student has a simple request – a transcript, a report card, how to do something like get a new metro card or find a locker.

In this case, all requests could be satisfied on the spot. This is what the student needs.

Caseloads are large. Imagine that you went into somebody's office and they were engaged in a conversation and the person you wanted to talk to smiled and nodded to you, held her hand up to the person she was taking to and said, "just a minute," and then gave her attention to you and asked what it was you came in for. How would you feel? Respected and acknowledged. The usual response to a student who walks into this situation is "Can't you see I'm talking," of "Don't interrupt," or "I'm busy, come back later" (in a curt tone) or just ignoring the student entirely and waving them away briskly.

In the time it takes to say any of the above, you can find out what a person wants and at the same time be a model for how kind people behave. This lesson, in my opinion, far outweighs "don't interrupt people when they are talking lesson." The person you were initially talking to has the confidence that the conversation is going to continue and also learns a valuable lesson.

Sometimes a conflict develops when the Deans feel that the counselor should make the initial call reporting bad behavior. Totally inappropriate. But the parents have to be informed. How to compromise? The deans make the first call since they are best able to explain why the student is being suspended and answer all questions the parent surely will have about the incident. Since the dean was actually involved in whatever the incident was the dean has thorough first-hand knowledge. This is something the parent deserves since they will be upset about their son or daughter's behavior and want, also, to be assured that there was fairness in what transpired.

The guidance counselor is effective in the follow-up conference once the suspension is over. In this subsequent conversation with parent and student, what is getting in the way of the student acting appropriately is discussed as well as how to take advantage of what the school has to offer – "an education that leads to graduating on time."

Here, the element of discovery is critical. A sensitive nonthreatening approach by the Counselor (or best of all the Principal of the school) lets the student lower their guard so that they can evaluate their own behavior. This takes some time to do – but really the same amount of time as the lecture method used by deans.

When a student is suspended and comes in with his or her family for a post-suspension conference, what is the goal of such a meeting? Of course the parents and the counselor will review academics, attendance and graduation requirements. The parents will have a chance to read what the teachers are saying about the student and will come away from the meeting with a lot of beneficial information. No doubt the student and parent will sign an agreement about how the student is going to conform to appropriate school behavior and carry a behavior sheet to be signed by each teacher each period of the day so that their parents can review it every evening and sign it. The goal of this meeting goes back to "discovery." Once the student is self-aware, it is clear to them what behavioral changes are necessary.

The goal of the technique used by the counselor is that the student "discovers" what it is that he or she did in terms of consequences and responsibility

A guidance counselor is licensed by the New York State Education Department and is thoroughly familiar with all the requirements for graduation and the intricacies of the regulations issued by New York State. The counselor also has a vast knowledge of educational alternatives. This conversation is the perfect opportunity to cement the link between scholarship and behavior and go on to focus on graduating on time and future plans.

STRATEGIES USED BY

GUIDANCE COUNSELORS

It is wise to conduct a lengthy meeting with the families of students who are failing just about everything for the second year in a row and who would benefit by transferring to another school. During such a conference, you want the parents and the student to "discover" that transferring is the best course to take. You do not want to leave anyone with the feeling that they are being "kicked out."

ATTENDANCE

In 2002, more than 12 years ago, Betsy Gotbaum wrote a critical report about high schools. She said, based on her statistics, that thousands of students were being pushed out of their high schools and urged to go to alternative schools or pursue GED programs. She said it appeared more students were discharged to other programs than were graduated. She said that school administrators were not making it clear to students and their parents that students have a right to remain in their school until age 21.

Betsy Gotbaum said enough wasn't being done to help students who need academic intervention. She thought school counselors ought to meet with these students and their families and play a role in really helping students who are failing.

Now the hard part about all of this is that schools are judged on their attendance rates and the number of Long Term Absentees (LTAs) on their rosters. Betsy Gotbaum's report is in the abstract. Were we to make it a personal report about a specific student who has been continually absent, we have to ask, "Does the school really want the student to remain in the school they're in?

The quick answer appears to be "no" because the student and others just like the student are dragging down the attendance rates. It is not in the Principal's interest to have such students remain in the building.

Let's say it's November 1st of the school term and a student is wooed back into school by her counselor with genuine assistance from the attendance teacher (the old truant officer) and the student's parents. In three weeks it will be Thanksgiving. The student has missed most of the assignments since the beginning of September. When the student returns to class at this time, many teachers will make negative comments drawing unwanted focus to someone who is sensitive to begin with (namely, this failing absentee who has been convinced by all in an effort that began in September to come back to school). Is there any teacher who would unobtrusively make the student feel welcome and later on after class make him or her feel welcome?

The usual comments by teachers are: "Sooooo, you decided to drop in?" or "You don't think you're going to pass this class, do you?" And despite the fact that it is a New York State law that students must come to school everyday, the teachers believe for the most part that the guidance department "LET" the student come back.

Now, teachers are under the gun to have large percentages of students pass their classes and also pass the Regents examinations. So are the Principals. Without high Regents passing rates and high rates of promotion, a school is in danger of receiving a failing grade from the Mayor.

With regard to attendance, there comes a time, usually at 16-1/2 and closer to 17 that a maturity bell rings and these problem students are ready to make a positive academic change. They are ready and want to transfer to an alternative high school and seriously try to graduate. OR, they buckle down knowing that it will take an extra year or year- and- a- half to graduate in their own school.

They are psychologically and age ready to apply to City-As-School, Satellite and many other transfer schools and they have enough credits to meet the admissions pre-requisite.

At this time, a guidance counselor is a wonderful resource -- someone who knows which schools accept which students. She meets with the student's family and makes the appointments for these students at the school they are eligible to apply to. She can walk them through the steps. And this is greatly appreciated. The student does not feel "pushed out" at all. They are being helped to finally get an education in a school that is right for them. Countless hours of contact have been made with such a family leading up to this decision. The student and parents have not been neglected by the school in the years preceding this decision. But the options were not available to them in their sophomore year at age 15.

If a school if in need of improvement (a designation given by the Mayor), then all students in the school are eligible to transfer. Their parents automatically receive a packet of information and they are invited to select 10 schools of interest and mail the form back. Unfortunately, many parents are overwhelmed by this large envelope and ignore it or store it away not taking advantage of the offer.

What can be offered to a 15-and-a-half-year-old student who has spent freshman and sophomore year already miserably? They should be juniors but don't have enough credits to be juniors (21 credits). They have between 8 credits or 9 credits, sometimes 12 credits or 15 credits.

SCHOOL-WIDE SOLUTION

If the school is intent upon "pushing these students out" because they are simply ruining attendance and promotion statistics at the crucial period when the school is being observed by the City and the State, then, in my opinion, it is up to management to actively participate by dev eloping a step-by-step list (like a recipe) of interventions. At certain points -- say quarter-way, half-way and at the end -- the Principal ought to be present at these meetings to lend gravitas and know-how to the proceedings. It would also change the working conditions climate to one of cooperation and working together toward a shared goal for management and counselors.

ATTENDANCE SOLUTIONS

Junior Year Abroad -- That is something successful suburban students are accustomed to. They go to a foreign country, say France or Kenya, for example, and live with a family in that country for six months to a year learning the language and living away from home, developing independence and learning how to adapt in a foreign setting. They receive high school credits for that term.

This concept might be applied to sophomores who are failing again and again. Why not let these students have a "sophomore year abroad" for a term or a year, perhaps as a guest in a Charter School or in a program where you learn on-line accumulating enough credits to be a senior upon returning to the home school. Provision would have to be made during this time for intensive study so that their English, Global and U.S. History Regents have been taken and passed before returning to their home school or offering an alternative testing method for these three regents.

Such students appear to need an alternative method of instruction.

PROGRAMMING SOLUTIONS

Students are so grateful for the opportunity to reverse a failing grade that their whole attitude toward school changes. They feel they are being acknowledged. They feel they are cared about and now they take an interest at 15 years of age in being promoted even though they failed miserably the first time. Parents become the school's ally. In our school, if you fail one or two classes in the first term of the freshman year, you are permitted to take credit recovery. But if you have been absent from most of your classes, you are denied this opportunity. How can you recover a class you never really took? This is also a motivator to do better. The standard is that when you fail,

an automatic green light does not go on for recovery. You
need a minimum grade of 55.

O! YOU KNOW MY NAME!

What is the most showy way a guidance counselor
can let a student know she recognizes a student as a person
who matters? Being able to say hello with his or her name
when you see a student in the hallway, or when he or she
walks into your office or sees you in the street.

"O! You know my name. Smile. (Or if they are
with two other students from school, one of them will more
than likely say, "She knows your name!")

Right there you've made an important connection
so that your advice has import (tutoring, buying an alarm
clock that works, for example).

Is the guidance counselor able to get to know
everyone's name easily? Well, you needn't have lengthy
conferences all the time. But short frequent meetings are

the key as well as brief visits to one or two classes on a regular basis. How I miss homeroom. That was a period built into the school day where counselors had the opportunity to communicate with students on a regular basis.

MATH

How can we interest students in math when no one can understand what is being taught?

Does it have to be this way? The freshmen in my caseload who take math generally fail it in the first marking period. A great number fail the course completely at the end of the term and will have to repeat it – and sometimes repeat it and repeat it and repeat it before advancing to the next math course.

How prepared are students to tackle Algebra? How does the school address this recurring situation? Does a maturity alarm bell have to go off before an understanding of algebra is possible? Can anything but intensive one-on-one tutoring suffice?

The best math teachers understand exactly what it is that students cannot grasp – the stumbling block. These teachers offer a variety of explanations for the same concept so that the student will catch on. They say that each student has a particular learning style and that when the learning style of the student matches the teaching style of the teacher, there will be success for the student. The teacher who is aware of how various students learn can be successful with a vast number of students with different learning styles. They are the best teachers and the teachers whose classes are most in demand by the students.

Now, let's look at math itself. It is taught like a foreign language that nobody is speaking. What is wrong with business math, especially in a high school where the majors are Information Systems, Accounting, Legal Studies, Computer Science, Marketing and Travel and Tourism?

Wouldn't it be better to teach students how to solve math problems that they encounter in everyday life? What's wrong with teaching math in a way that relates to the other subjects the students are taking? What is wrong with offering a math class devoted to investments and stocks? What is wrong with solving for x in situations that occur frequently? What is wrong with using mastery as a test for advancement rather than grades -- in math?

Every year, when the senior class ranking list is published in school, I ask students who come to my guidance office to look at the ranking list and tell me where they stand on the list, if they are in the top ten percent of the graduates. Stares. Stares. These are students with 80, 85 90 cumulative averages. I ask students if they are in the top half of their graduating class. Stares.

FOREIGN LANGUAGE

Students are required to take one year of a foreign language. In a city like New York, where so many people speak Spanish and where directional signs and ads on the subway are translated into Spanish, where there are Spanish shows on television, where there are local papers in Spanish and English, students have a wonderful opportunity to learn a foreign language from a speaker's point of view.

Here an opportunity for students to learn the language the way a child does (or an immigrant) through learning the ABCs first, numbers second and interesting phrases and sentences next so that grammar is absorbed through repetition of conversation. There is no reason to continue the old way of conjugating verbs. And since there are so many Dominican and Puerto Rican students in the freshman class, they certainly can be pared with African American, European (white) and Asian students in class to stimulate conversation. Exercises in spelling, accentuations, idioms and verb formation can be briefly taught by the teacher.

Another useful foreign language is Sign Language. This is a very practical language choice that students would have pride in mastering. What's the problem with recognizing it as a language other than English spoken?

HISTORY

Recently, I asked one of the teachers of U.S. History if he geared any lessons to Black History since we just celebrated Black History month. His response was that that idea was "old hat" and that we've progressed beyond that.

Then later that morning I was having a discussion with two students in my office. I asked one if he lived in Manhattan. He said no he lived in Harlem and the other student said the rest of Manhattan was mainly white and that Harlem was African American. I said what about The Heights? He said, "Dominicans live there." So much for old hat!

But have we yet acknowledged that African Americans were pioneers in this country? I believe the American History curriculum ought to be changed to focus on American History from a black history perspective. Not "Black History Month" as something divorced from "regular history," but taught either strictly from a new perspective. There could be a class on landmark Supreme Court cases centering on black issues tied to the history of the time. It's hard to give up a European focus. I believe all students ought to learn the African National Anthem, just as we recognize Le Marseilles and know "The Star Spangled Banner." Could the subject of the Holocaust be taught in conjunction with Slavery.

Wouldn't it be interesting to read certain articles in the The Amsterdam News with the same subject articles from the The New York Times?

ENGLISH

Keep Shakespeare. Add Henry Gates and other great African American and Latino authors. Drop F. Scott Fitzgerald and Hawthorne. In Shakespeare, the emotional entanglements are biblical in proportion and the poetry unique and superlative. Teachers could inform the class that they have to read the first 10 pages carefully at home because they will be called on to read aloud in class. Before students read aloud, the teacher could go over the vocabulary that is difficult.

HANDS ON CURRICULUM

For 7th and 8th graders, the students need a hands on curriculum. Pre-teens like to connect facts with action, for the most part. They would do better not sitting in classrooms the entire day.

BARBARA CHRISTEN

Barbara Christen (1974-1989), the founding Principal of Murry Bergtraum, established the fine reputation of the school with business links and active support of the Downtown Business Community -- Chase, Estee Lauder, accounting and law firms, all of whom have programs with our school. Representatives from these and other Wall Street companies met regularly with our principal and assistant principals. They offered mentoring through their companies, internships, and donate office furniture and computers to our school.

ELSIE CHAN

SCHOOL SPIRIT A LA MURRY BERGTRAUM HIGH SCHOOL

Great school spirit in Murry Bergtraum was initiated and developed under the leadership of Elsie Chan when she was Principal (1990-1997). She wasn't afraid to have assemblies. She didn't worry that students might get unruly in the enclosed space of the auditorium. She encouraged the Puerto Rican and Dominican students to put on dance acts that reflected the way teenagers dance -- to our generation gap adult eyes -- wildly, suggestive and in skinny skirts and decolte tops.

The audience was ecstatic, jumping up and down in their seats and applauding and whistling but they were never anything but well mannered. These assemblies had dance acts performed by the Student Organization (SO), the African Student Union (step dancing like you've never seen before -- T-O-P-S) and ethnic contributions by the Asian and Indian Clubs.

Once the Asian Club had invited a professional, classical Chinese Fan Dance Troupe for the Chinese New Year Assembly. They were superb and this teenage audience appreciated their artistry.

But let someone sing off-key or be too corny -- they were booed off the stage.

Within a short time after Elsie Chan became principal, she orchestrated the "silent fire drill." Her goal, which became the school's goal, was to have 3,000 students leave the school building when the gongs rang in total silence and return in total silence when the return gongs sounded. Some faculty members laughed and thought it was silly. Others thought it couldn't be done.

Here's how she did it. The school had practice fire drills floor by floor. She started with the fourth floor. Each teacher in each classroom instructed their students about how to behave in a fire drill. They were told they would be suspended if they spoke a word. Then, on a particular day, the fourth floor and only the fourth floor walked through the drill, down the stairs and outside. The teachers did not speak to each other during this drill. However, the teachers already knew where they were to be positioned in advance of this drill. Then when the fourth floor students were lined up across in the triangle on Madison and Pearl Streets and on Avenue of the Finest (in back of the school in the shadow of the Brooklyn Bridge), Elsie Chan in her high heels and polka dot suit ran by the lined up students and silently waved and told them how good they were. This was repeated on successive days with the third floor, the second floor and then the first floor. The guidance counselors, assistant principals and others who worked on the main floor and did not have students were drilled on another day so that they knew where exactly to stand in the street, which door to hold open or in which direction to waive students.

So when the big day came for the real fire drill for the entire school, the students in each classroom throughout the building had been informed in small classroom groups as to exactly what to do and had one practice run already.

Elsie Chan in her high heels ran by the "troops" and silently waived to all and told them "silently" thumbs up. Woe to the rare students who spoke. A showy suspension. As for the rest of the school? Passersby marveled that 3,000 students could be quiet at one time.. Each succeeding fire drill was totally silent. This principal took a small task and made the whole school proud at its accomplishment. It should be noted here that this practice was essential on 9/11. We could see the planes crash into the Word Trade Center from the back door of our school. Listening quietly to loudspeaker instructions on that day was crucial.

The next overall change made by Elsie was the expansion of the student government -- from a 34 member group of high academic achievers whose academic averages were at least 90 per cent and whose activities centered on fundraising -- into an organization welcoming and encouraging all students. A high average was no longer a pre-requisite. The Principal felt that many students who were not doing well academically had other talents that would make them excellent members of the student organization. The new head of this endeavor was Ada Colon, a teacher with the respect and love of the students, a winning M.C. at student assemblies, a fair disciplinarian who never shied away from a good verbal argument while maintaining the affection of the students (They called her "Ma."). Ms. Colon knew the value of arguing with students. She allowed them to speak up -- and to win when fair. She was also a natural delegator so that students were in charge of all bulletin boards throughout the school and all sound and lighting at assemblies.

The student organization spearheaded the school's recycling program -- collecting filled recycling bags regularly and supplying new ones. They were also the ushers at assemblies and earned a credit as a student in the leadership class. When a guidance counselor or teacher needed help, they gladly stepped up. The S.O. coordinated the mentoring programs with the Downtown Business Association whereby students throughout the school were paired up with mentors at Chase Manhattan Bank for example. Then, a regular fundraising effort was added on so that there were visible fund-raising drives for disaster victims. Tables were set up in the lobby for Haiti and the Dominican Republic.

The S. O. transformed the school lobby for parent teacher conferences from a hushed affair to one with coffee and cake for parents and the sale of beauty products from our school's Este Lauder/Clinique boutique.

Elsie also established the morning muster where Security Officers, APs of guidance, organization and security, the Head of Security (called Level 3) and the Principal met to go over any problems that were occurring, hot issues and potential problems.

Another school wide glue was introduced -- the Weekly calendar with "real information" on it -- fire drills, class trips, Principal's Cabinet Meetings, department and faculty meeting dates. Elsie wanted everybody to know everything and by the force of her personality and wiles she was successful.

Before Elsie, when a student returned to school after a one to five day suspension, the AP of Guidance (in lieu of the Principal as stated by official regulations) met with the parent and child for a follow-up discussion.

Elsie Chan wanted a team to participate in this meeting to give it gravitas. So, the AP of guidance, the student's guidance counselor, the AP of the student's major (say, Information Systems) and any teachers involved in the suspension (if they were free) were required to participate at these meetings. The guidance counselor had an opportunity to review the student's transcript with the parent and group and to have a plan "a contract" to suggest and provisions to be initiated (behavior sheet) which would be signed by the student and his or her parent and the AP of guidance and the guidance counselor.

Elsie published a monthly attendance statement that compared the Houses attendance numbers for each grade and the number of students. She wanted the guidance counselors to be able to rattle off statistics (how many freshman, how many Long Term Absentees, how many students in the school.)

Overall, Elsie Chan was a leader and through the force of her personality and the threat of "going to the pen" which she rarely did , the school changed in a significant way. You could say it had the spirit of a private school. Her door was open. The worst students and the troublemakers loved her. She took pride in the graduation rate and helped students in any way she could. The faculty stayed out of her path. The intractable problem was "cutters."

GRACE JULIEN

Our next Principal, Grace Julien (1997 -- 2002) didn't go for suggestive dancing by the students. However, though she was very N-E-R-V-O-U-S about large congregations of students, she knew the importance of assemblies and supported them and came to every one of them.

Grace Julien had the music teacher write a school song and it is sung at graduation every year through June, 2010 -- after which we needed school spirit more than ever.

Cutters, hall walkers, distracting influences in class, this was the formidable task that Grace Julien successfully dealt with. She appointed an Assistant Principal of Security who was not afraid to take the bull by the horns and get rid of this kind of behavior. He insisted that the parents of students "acting out" attend as many conferences as it took to bring about change. He had the know-how to scare many a student straight.

The Principal worked closely with Ada Colon, the popular Coordinator of the Student Organization to engage problem students.

Ms. Julien had an open door policy and she greeted the students at the front door on many a day. Ms. Julien complimented the students. She was loved by the faculty.

The Principal thought it important that we have a strong college office and have as many students as possible strive for the best colleges. She knew who got scholarships and wanted as many students as possible to apply to college.

Grace Julien was math A.P. for many years in Murry Bergtraum. It was in the tradition of the school to foster genuine talent from within. She led the school on 9/11 and what followed.

BARBARA ESMILLA

Our fourth Principal was Barbara Esmilla (2002-2010) whose tenure coin-sided with the first eight years of Mayor Bloomberg's becoming the head of the Department of Education. Ms. Esmilla suffered because she had to toe the line and concentrate on raising the promotion rate (60 per cent of the grade of her school's evaluation), making sure English and Math grades matched the passing percentage the Mayor established for our school and making sure that class instruction followed certain requirements. It appeared that Ms. Esmilla was completely beleagured by the Department of Educations' dictum to improve the 9th grade promotion rate. The fact that Barbara Esmilla was the New York City Commissioner of Sports previously and our school was number one in girls varsity basketball in the five boroughs and continued to be during her tenure with colleges such as Rutgers recruiting heavily from our school DID NOT MATTER. Our college efforts lost their special place. The fact that our students were being accepted by Syracuse and NYU did n't have any value either. In addition, our college scholarship program was a non-factor in the school improvement equation. All the things that came into flower under Elsie Chan and Grace Julien fell by the wayside because they did not matter to City Hall. Just promotional rate.

When Barbara Esmilla addressed the faculty, she was open and honest with the staff, sharing her feelings and all information about the status of our school and hinting that she often felt the way the faculty did about the new way of doing things (required by the Mayor and Chancellor Klein), but she helped us see that we had to do things a new way if we wanted our school to survive.

**CHANGES MADE**

During the September 2003 to June, 2004 school year, Ms. Esmilla felt pressured by "the powers that be" to change the school structure to indicate that we were dealing with our low promotion rate (60% of the grade given to a school by the Mayor and the Chancellor) and poor instructional focus. Ms. Esmilla told the faculty that we had to do something to show we were tackling our problems.

So in the Fall (September) of 2004, the Small Learning Community structure was begun (after a year of planning and feeling in limbo). During the previous Spring term (February, 2004 to June, 2004), Murry Bergtraum's faculty and guidance counselors and social workers were being primed for the "New Structure." Teachers were asked to "sign on" if they wanted to participate in the design and teach in one of the Small Learning Communities (SLCs). The Principal and Assistant Principal had lengthy meetings each week to flesh out the design. I remained guidance counselor of the new Information Systems/Computer Science House.

Unfortunately, something happened. The Mayor and Chancellor Klein gave the impression that they barely tolerated teachers and counselors and were suspicious of everyone's ability to do anything.

Barbara Esmilla retired in 2010, eight years later when our school received a C rating followed by a D the next year. Word went out that Murry Bergtraum High School was no longer a "good school." Parents routinely asked, "Is Murry Bergtraum closing." We were no longer perceived as THE school that parents and students vied to attend.

Yet, our school remained number one in the city in girls varsity basketball -- a tribute to Barbara Esmilla. Our students are still courted by the top college teams. We had a tennis team, volley ball team, track team, boxing and boys varsity basketball. And we had a strong liaison with Syracuse University thanks to our College Advisor.

Barbara Esmilla started her career as a teacher under Barbara Christen. She went on to become a loved Senior Advisor and then an A.P. of Guidance (though at another school) before returning to her dear Bergtraum as unanimously elected Principal of the school. She encouraged graduates to return as teachers and hired as many guidance counselors as possible. She saw their value.

REPUTATION OF MURRY BERGTRAUM

Murry Bergtraum is a school for business careers. When students in the 8th grade in JHS decide to apply to our school, they choose one of our majors such as Information Systems Technology, Accounting, Computer Science, Marketing, Legal Studies among others. Just like LaGuardia High School where students choose drama, music or dance when they begin their 9th grade classes.

The school offers a strong college program -- offering AP Calculus, AP English, AP Science, AP History as they study the major they were accepted for.

Our school is large and lovely. We have up-to-date software and learn Word, Excel, Access and Web design. We have such features as a school store completely decorated and stocked with Estee and Clinque products supplied by the Estee Laudeer cosmetics company who underwrites the marketing program. In fact, all of Murry Bergtraum 's majors have the support of the Downtown Business community of Lower Manhattan (Wall Street) and they provide school year and summer internships to students who receive a stipend from the company. This work component is called Co-op, where the students get the hands-on supervised business experience for which they are paid a stipend.

Once a term, men and women successful in their professions (many of them Bergtraum graduates) are invited o speak to various classes about the field they work in and what path lead them there.

FEAR OF BEING FIRED

There is a fear of being fired and an awareness of being too old emanating from our Senior citizen Mayor and former Chancellor Klein. For those past eight years, whenever a member of the Mayor's Region Office in Manhattan made a presentation or conducted staff development for our school, they appeared to be shivering in their shoes. They just about always remarked "If I still have my job." And there were far too many remarks smacking of ageism.

It's great to be able to fire people who disagree with you and to surround yourself with employees who help the boss achieve his or her vision. Things run so smoothly for the boss when people work long hours as well, without overtime pay. It is so cheerful for a boss who is 65+ to choose eager teachers who have recently completed their Master's Degrees in teaching. It's great to be a senior citizen Chancellor -- Chancellor Klein -- and feel that age has given you wisdom and know-how and competence.

And what a savings to focus on teachers with seniority, portraying them as a bunch of talentless hangers-on. And to give Principals just enough funds to make it cost effective to not hire teachers and guidance counselors with seniority so that the pool of excessed teachers has more and more senior members who can't get jobs and then to characterize those teachers as "someone no-one wants to hire." Of course Principals don't want to hire them. They cost too much when you can get two new teachers for salary of one senior teacher.

Just think. Our 70 year old mayor extended term limit so that he could run for a third term (12 years all together) and squeeze out the opportunity for a younger person (Christine Quinn, the President of the City Council) to run for Mayor.

One of the drawbacks of peopling the Department of Education mainly with newcomers is that they are at a loss to offer advice -- so that no one is in charge to answer procedural and technical questions about State of Education law as if pertains to academic questions.

One thing that is kept rather quiet is how each new small high school or charter school selects its students? It would be interesting to know student-by-student, school by school how they were selected. It would be interesting to know the steps these new schools take to deal with teenagers who present a serious distraction in the classroom.

In my school, there was one particular student who was placed in our school in the middle of the term. (He had disciplinary problems in his former school and the region office told our school that he had to be accepted.) This student was on medication for mood and he was reluctant to take it. The consequence was that he would sleep at his desk and/or suddenly walk around the classroom muttering.

One day, when an extremely talented social studies teacher was scheduled to be reviewed during the region's analysis of our school (which was part of the grade we would get from the Department of Education), this student was wisked away from the class before it started. How would this teacher have been evaluated with such conduct going on in her class? Isn't good student management the prelude to good teaching?   Though this student was clearly a case for the Deans, the Assistant Principal of the Department asked his guidance counselor "as a special favor" to keep him in her office for the period. This meant cancelling a group meeting with five juniors who were looking forward to the meeting. How good was that for enhancing the image of the counselor? What if being asked to cancel student meetings at the drop of a hat were a frequent occurrence for counselors? How good is that for portraying the counselor as someone you can rely on? The student, who had to be looked after constantly, asked to go back to his class and it was the task of the counselor to distract him from this idea for 45 minutes.

We are a large high school and many fear the top resource (a kind way of saying dumping ground) for countless troublemakers from other schools that the Principal is required to accept by the Department of Education all though the term. Would such a student be placed in one of the small new high schools that are such models of learning?

ASKING QUESTIONS

It is also understood by the Mayor's staff in the Department of Education that a faculty member or guidance counselor cannot question a directive from the Mayor without quickly being put down because no one is allowed to acknowledge any difficulty. Therefore, you are on your own when two directive conflict with each other. No one feels safe to "be real," meaning to acknowledge that a request seems quite impossible to carry out without making something else less of a priority. Employees of the Region must parrot their directives -- Period . This is the antithesis of a good education and good citizenship which encourages thinking, questioning and arguing.

CHARTER SCHOOLS

Just as it is wonderful for a boss to hand pick his or her employees, so it is just the ticket to success for Charter Schools and new small schools to hand pick their students, which they do.

Are we making believe that three or four or five separate high schools can share the same space (on different floors) and all get along? Do these high school students magically fly to their assigned space once they enter the building at 8 a.m.? Or do they have to interact with each other? The teacher I spoke to said in her charter school, the lunchroom and gym are shared by at least two other schools. This is a nightmare.

Has the Department of Education forgotten about the American capitalist tradition of competition and exclusivity? Sharing is not high on the list of major corporations. Are we not basing our new school structure on the business model? Isn't "making nice" a feature of kindergarten?

Let's look at LaGuardia and Martin Luther King High Schools when they first opened. The students couldn't get along with each other on the way to school or at three o'clock even though they were in two SEPARATE large traditional high school buildings across the street from each other.

It may seem to some that we are moving toward a model where the idea that art and culture and space and the act of experimentation in science and discussion in history detract from "the message" of school testing in math and reading. Sounds like Chairman Mao to some. Is it petty and selfish to want art rooms and laboratories and rehearsal space?

Looking back, Murry Bergtraum under our first Principal, Barbara Christen, had an A-one reputation for the longest time precisely because students chose our school and, of course, the school was free of laws to restrict it from hand-picking exactly whom they wanted. Students who were eager to study Computer Science applied to the school in the thousands and those with outstanding attendance and outstanding math grades were likely to be selected by the Principal and Assistant Principals. No one forced the school to take students based on a statistical formula. But it seems, the Department of Education went from one extreme to the other -- from hand picking students to having a lotto select 50% of the student body. Even if students with lower averages on the statistical scale were given the opportunity to attend BUT were selected by Murry Bergtraum's administration, it would immediately have a positive impact on school performance. During Barbara Christen's tenure, this school, which had about 2,000 students, at that time, had an over 90 per cent attendance rate in the computer science major -- before 50% of the student body was selected at random.

WHAT STAYED THE SAME

Our school always had 9 business majors, i.e. Computer Science, Information Systems, Accounting, Marketing, Legal Studies, etc. and students stayed in the major for 4 years (think of Music and Art High School or Performing Arts High School). Those students, like ours, came into the school knowing that they were going to major in Music or Art or Drama or Dance for four years along with their academic subjects -- just as Murry

Bergtraum's students had chosen Information Systems or Computer Science, etc. before they stepped into the building the first day or school.

So, the Small Learning Community (SLC) focus was a natural for our school. We already had the majors that became the basis or theme for the Small Learning Communities. The big change was that each Small Learning Community would have teachers who taught ONLY in one learning community. For example, each Small Learning Community (or major or academy) had a math teacher, a science teacher, a history teacher, an English teacher who only taught the students in their SLC. Each community had a Director who was also an Assistant Principal of a particular discipline (Math AP; English AP., etc.). All the students in a particular SLC (say the Information Systems SLC) had their lunch period at the same time so that the teachers and guidance counselor were free to meet together each day (during the students' lunch period) with their Director to talk about issues they had with students, plans for activities, and plan instructional development. It seemed like we were a little private school within a large public high school. If a student had a discipline problem, all the teachers could meet with the students and their parents at once during this period.

As for the guidance counselors, they were each associated with one Academy as they had been with one major previously and had those students from their Freshmen to their Senior year.

All the students in a particular major or SLC were in classes with each other only. There were approximately three classes of Freshmen in each Academy (102 students).

The guidance counselor had access to the students because these teachers welcomed visits and allowed students to go to the counselor's office when the counselor sent passes for them.

If a school has enough money and space to provide teachers for this structure, then no teacher would have to double and teach outside of his or her Small Learning Community. If a school had enough space, then the Small Learning Community could also be together geographically on a particular floor or part of a particular floor in the building. Programming, to a large extent, would be do-able.

So what is the difference between having 5 schools in a large high school building facility like Murry Bergtraum's and having Small Learning Communities housed in such a building?

PLENTY.

The students in the Small Learning Communities are united by the fact that they all are students of MBHS and belong in the entire building. No other students from "another school" are walking up and down the stairways, sharing the lunchroom, sharing the gym. The school is

united by having one Principal shared by all -- not 4
separate Principals as with 4 small independent schools in
a building. There is more collegiality in one large high
school.

THE FIRST YEAR OF SLCs

For the first year of this change, the Information
Systems SLC was lucky enough to have a Director who
knew how to work with teachers and with the guidance
counselor in a collegial way. When we met daily, we sat at
a large round table in our own office space. We were free
to express our opinions and many times the Director
changed his plan to reflect how the teachers felt. There was
a lot of input.

The Director scheduled outings for the SLC from
the get-go so that the 9th grade students in the Information
Systems SLC could bond with each other and the teachers
and guidance counselor. We went to the Body Museum in

the South Street Seaport and two other sites. Going to a site in the school's neighborhood opened the eyes of most of the students as to how close to the South Street Seaport our school was. The three classes in this initial SLC had rotating trips on different days.

The Director also arranged for the students to see a new pre-Broadway show, "In the Heights," a show set in Upper Manhattan and focusing on the Latino community there, a neighborhood where many of the Dominican and Puerto Rican students lived.

We also had an after school roundtable activity once a week with refreshments (pizza, soda, chips) supplied by the guidance counselor, where the Director led a focused discussion. In the beginning, only three or four students showed up (and not the top achievers). As we went along, there were 10 or 12 regulars. These students welcomed an outlet to be heard and recognized.

Because there was so much work involved for the A.P. doubling as a Director of the SLC, this talented Director chose not to continue the next year. He offered to remain as Director of the SLC with someone else taking on the task of AP of English. This idea was rejected by the Principal. She said the "order" from the Region Superintendent required the Director to wear 2 hats -- that of AP of a department and SLC Director.

One drawback of the new systems was that teachers felt it was difficult for the same students to be with each other all day long. They were harder to discipline because they knew each other so well. Many of the students did not like the idea of being with the same group of students day in and day out. The beauty of a regular large high school is variety.

Teachers also had to devote a lot of time to this endeavor. While there was incentive "per session" funds to compensate them for some of this extra time -- it hardly covered the many, many hours put in day in and day out.

We have a union. Otherwise, these teachers could have been fired if they did not do tremendous overtime WITHOUT being compensated as in many charter schools.

The guidance counselor had an opportunity to meet with students in small groups on a rotating basis and really give them the opportunity to ask questions, to seek answers to questions that were important to them, to air grievances and hear how other students dealt with particular problems. The counselor was free to make brief classroom visits for timely announcements.

A discussion of graduation requirements will not really sink in unless discussed individually or in a small group. Entering a class of 34 new students and rattling off the requirements is not guidance. It needs a small group setting where Freshmen can ask for clarification, a setting that permits the unasked questions to be brought up without the risk of ridicule that asking in class may bring. The guidance counselor can bring up the unasked question and lead the group to a wanted discussion

PROFESSIONAL DEVELOPMENT (PD)

It was determined that the guidance counselors needed to learn how to use Excel spreadsheets and Professional Development (PD) was designated for this. We were handicapped by never having learned to use said technology. November 2nd, Election Day was the next date set aside for PD.

For some reason, Professional Development was hastily called together during the Thursday before November 2nd during a regular class period. This is how it was conducted.

At the beginning of 7th period (a 45 minute long period), the counselors assembled in one of our computer rooms so that we could all sit at a computer while receiving instruction. The A.P. of Math was the instructor. For the first 15 minutes of the session, he and the techies were trying to get the overhead monitors to work so that the Math A.P. could demonstrate the steps on his large screen as we sat at our computers. That's 45 minutes minus 15 = 30 minutes left.

Then our passwords and IDs did not gain us entry so that the A.P. had to use his administrator's password at each of our monitors in order for us to log on. 25 minutes left.

Then, there was not a word acknowledging a ridiculous situation, meaning the words on the large monitor were so tiny that no one could read them as he pointed to them. It was so make believe.

But to our utter surprise, we were not being taught Excel. Instead, we were taught how to view data on a very long ARIS spreadsheet.

There I was again, like the little elementary, junior high school and high school Marcia who couldn't catch on. Not only that, as things were pointed out, I couldn't see them fast enough.

The A.P. explained that "SOME OF US" were able to learn technology faster than others (referring to the one guidance counselor who already knew this material) and that he had NO TIME to give us one-on-one instruction.

Certainly, what was meant to be daylong instruction was squeezed into 25 minutes with the handicaps enumerated above.

Once again, the administration felt it had provided "necessary training."

To analyze this situation vis-a-vis how students are taught, this was an example of "you really should have had groundwork in this technology or math or science of whatever subject you want to fill in, so that you could grasp what was being taught."

Nowhere is there acknowledgement that many, many, students, teachers and counselors are at the "below basic stage." And there is impatience BECAUSE it would take much longer to teach this group when there is no time because everyone has to take the "test" or "Regents" and meet the deadline.

Right before we were scheduled to learn Excel, we were given a large spread sheet assignment. This assignment was due before we had said P.D . Those counselors who handed their information -- but not in the Excel format -- were told to do it over. And do it over they did, getting assistance whichever way they could to put it in the Excel format. They then received a "U" rating for their first observation from the A.P. I was glad I already knew Excel.

OUR UNION -- THE UFT

You don't worry about whether you need the Union when things are going well. You take for granted the hard won negotiations that benefit in salary steps, the welfare plan, very low health benefit costs and due process (meaning you just can't be fired on the spot) and no layoffs in these hard times. Only a fool or someone basking in the glowing light of specialdom would not appreciate the efforts of the UFT.

You think you might even do without a Union if you have the "ear" of the chief. But there is a chasm so deep between management and labor at the moment, that any accusation by a Union member that Management many be using bullying tactics or getting away with lying with impunity forces management ranks to close. However, the Union is there for difficult times, which can be defined as the day it becomes clear who labor is and who management is and your position therein.

Since teachers are judged through the lens of favoritism, it is folly to think that teachers -- or counselors and everyone else -- will be treated fairly when it comes to being judged on "test scores" or so called "objective measures."

Who will teach the "well-behaved and best classes?" What about the students who are benefitting from a master teacher's expertise but are not up to the mark? Basing teachers' careers on scores will lead to more unhappiness and stress than any employee deserves because it does not reflect reality. What about receiving professional development to help you improve your class technique? How many professional developers are the "good friend teacher next door-type" who gave you great tips out of professional friendliness? Not any more. Those being helped by "professional developers" individually are frozen with fear because the PDs report right back to the Administration. Who, frozen with fear and looking forward to help in the form of a person reporting back to administration can develop. When you are genuinely being helped, you begin to flower. You learn.

DR. ANDREA LEWIS (Fall, 2010-Spring 2012)

Placed in the school by the Mayor to whip it into shape in 3 years for a bonus fee of $25,000. The Mayor wanted Dr. Lewis there to make sure the Regents Exam scores, graduation rate and promotion rate went up-up-up. She left after two years with a D-grade for the school (again!) and an F for school atmosphere. She did not lose her position with the Department of Education. Where is she now?

To improve literacy, Dr. Lewis wanted the school to be print rich. She did not approve of artwork displays or pictures on the 4 floors of extensive bulletin boards. She favored printed matter. Our outstanding art Program had to hide its light under a bushel -- or else!

The next "innovation" by Dr. Lewis was dropping the two majors that Murry Bergtraum is famous for: Computer Science and Information Systems (and excessing the teachers who taught them.) Who gets rid of Computers in this day and age when careers are based on them and students love to major in this area? These are majors that are springboards to successful careers followed by college.

Many of the students with Information Systems or Computer Science majors had no idea when they reached their sophomore year that their major was no longer in existence. There was an erosion of school spirit right here.

Dr. Lewis' appreciation of counselors can be illustrated by her end of the year "innovation" which barred most of the counselors from attending graduation and occupying their traditional place on the stage during the ceremony. She did this under the guise of work to be done.

(There wasn't any.)

LOTTE ALMONTE (Fall 2012 -

Selected by the Mayor to succeed Dr. Lewis, Lotte made no secret of her attitude toward counselor and by September 19, 2012 excessed 6 of the 7 counselors, each of whom had caseloads of approximately 300 students. The position of A.P. of Guidance was eliminated before the beginning of the school year. Also excessed were the AP Organization, the AP Security, the AP of Special Education, the AP of Foreign Language and the AP of ESL and Director of the Freshman House and the COSA.

Now, here is a question. Since everyone believes that Lotte was only doing what the Mayor wanted, why would the Mayor want to eliminate guidance? No reason was given to the counselors. In fact the Principal did not give the news to them. She had her AP Organization carry out the deed.

If you read the New York City Department of Education's website, you will read of the extensive responsibilities outlined by the DOE for counselors. You would think the DOE thought counselors were the most necessary professionals in a high school -- especially one with 1,800 students. But this is make-believe. Why did two Principals chosen by the Mayor have such negative attitudes toward guidance? Everyone asks: "Were they just following the Mayor's orders?" The school is not on the list to close nor was it being reorganized since it accepted a 9th grade class in September, 2012.

It is fair to say that plunking down two Principals who have no care about the school and the staff can only be ruinous to a school.

SCHOOL GRADES

When you are asked to weave straw into gold, you have to make a pact with the devil. For example, a school might suddenly restrict who can take the English Regents making certain that only those who can absolutely pass it sit for it. It's a way of boosting the passing rate for the school and a better observation for the Principal. Certain Principals require an 80% passing rate by teachers and call them to task if they don't comply. And we read about erasures on Uniform tests nationwide by Principals and Supervisors. Then there is also a tolerance of cheating.

ABOUT FIRST NAMES

The other day, a teacher sent a memo to the teachers with tips on writing a good recommendation.

In the memo, she gives an example of an effective paragraph using the name of "Ann Smith" as the student-example.

Let's switch to the Program Office where all of the students' programs and program changes are put together. One of the programmers was explaining something to an AP saying , "let's say 'Johnnny and Mary' need such-and-such on their programs."

Those aren't the names of the typical students who attend our school.   Citing Tamika or Shanice or Kiara or Dejon or Julio or Wei Wei points to a faculty member who has integrated reality.

DAILY GOINGS-ON

Guidance counselors are always trying to impress upon each other and everyone else about how busy they are. In graduate school, students taking their Master's in Guidance and Counseling were reminded quite often to "too their own horn." When Counselors speak to each other as they pass each other in the hallway, how very busy they are crops up in conversation.

When a teacher or Assistant Principal introduces the counselor to a class, they gush -- "this is the person who is there to help you. You can always go to your guidance counselor. She is there to help you." That phrase is a spoken guarantee for parents and students alike that in the Guidance Office is a guidance counselor who is always there when you wants a transcript printed or to look at your grades before the report cards reach your parent's mailbox (320 glances), to answer all telephone calls immediately and to meet with parents whenever they drop in -- with an appointment or not. She's the Guidance Fairy to give you what you want on the spot -- i.e. program changes because you don't like a teacher, or helping you one-third into the term to drop a course (AP bio) because you're finding it too difficult and it will ruin your average, or to answer questions such as app

lying for a fee waiver, a job, a new metro card. That phrase   portrays a counselor who can arrange lengthy conferences with the parent and student any time the parent desires to discuss "what is of concern."

I believe the reason counselors walk around endlessly emphasizing how busy they are, "tooting their own horn," comes from the sense that they are disappointing students and parents all day long when they are out of their offices troubleshooting with a student; conducting required counseling sessions, conducting post or pre-suspension conferences or attending small learning community meeting or Pupil Personnel Team meetings.

A LOOK AT GUIDANCE

For a Guidance Department to be a united, collegial and strong entity, it needs a   number of ingredients:

1) An Assistant Principal who has had a guidance background -- whether in social services, work programs or as a Coordinator of Student Services (COSA) -- who understands the huge scope of the job and who wants to be

instrumental in supporting and supervising the guidance staff.

2)   An Assistant Principal who insists that all the counselors are an integral part of the planning meetings for formulating the school's guidance program, the summer program, the recovery programs and arranges meetings with the individual department Assistant Principals (English, Science, Math, etc.) and the Programming Office for overviews and opportunities for questions. In this respect, the Assistant Principal of Guidance is an upholder of the counselors' Union contract which specifies that counselors be included in the planning of all guidance programs. In many schools, "knowledge is power" and the willingness to share that knowledge is stubbornly withheld from the top down.

3) An Assistant Principal who does not view "knowledge as power" as something to hoard and share only with favorites.

4) An Assistant Principal who gives the guidance staff the minutes of their monthly meetings as a tickler file to up-coming deadlines and as a handy guide to current activities and concerns.

5) An Assistant Principal who has respect for the inquires of her/his staff members and does not throw clarification for such inquiries back into the counselors' faces with a derisive, "Don't you know that already." This is not only an inability to supervise but another example of withholding know-how.

6) An Assistant Principal who can be relied upon as a supervisor one can ask for expertise and assistance in difficult cases and who offers such assistance uniformly to all guidance counselors.

HOW DOES MURRY BERGTRAUM

HIGH SCHOOL RATE GUIDANCE

WISE?

All of the features enumerated above have completely disappeared from the guidance program as the school undergoes one change after another in overall structure in its quest for high quality review ratings. It has reached the point where guidance counselors have been relegated to taking orders immediately -- without notice, with hardly any programming information (unless a counselor ferrets it out for themselves) and with a taboo against asking questions. They are treated like oarsmen in the hull of a ship -- as often depicted in old movies -- with a drum beater on watch beating out the rhythm of how fast the workers should "pull" while a slave master walks around to see that this is done.

This is a meaningless approach to programming that has led to counselors having to do programming "immediately" with hardly any notice only to be told after doing it that it has to be completely redone and redone and redone because some issues and information from the top have "changed everything." Consulting the counselors to begin would have avoided the necessity for do-overs. So fiercely are comments discouraged, they have been inhibited completely. Programming involves analysis of about 300 individual students as mentioned before. (Quiet time needed.)

At the same time, students want a counselor's attention all day long -- those with appointments and those who just drop in on the spur of the moment. It's the nature of the job. Here is where an Assistant Principal who understands the predicament the Department has been placed in can ameliorate the situation instead of "banging the drum."

A strong Assistant Principal knows that in guidance, the counselors (just as in social work) deal with unexpected and emergency professional situations all day long -- a runaway ... a very good student who is suddenly hospitalized with a diagnosis of a grave disease who wants school work immediately to help him or her mentally forge on by keeping up with current school work ... parents of LTAs (long term absentees) who just walk in and have to be acknowledged.

If you are under the supervision of an Assistant Principal who is not attuned to this reality and turns their back on this fact and simply honors deadlines, then C ounselors are working under unrelenting pressure -- terrible undermining of the professional guidance staff. It engenders students to endlessly complain because they, too, need constant attention (300 of them -- one at any time.)

Not being allowed to express one's judgment comes at a high price for counselors. For example, if a counselor can see correctly that it would be better to wait for Regents exam results and final June grades before programming students for summer school, they do so at the peril of their own stress level. Never mind that time tested experience shows that there will be enough time to do summer programming easily following those June grades since everything in the current method has to be done and redone and finally changed anyway once the grades and Regents results are in.

A vacuum exists where Assistant Principals -- say from Science or Social Studies -- who have no awareness of the deadlines -- issue complete programming orders for their subjects and imperiously send them to counselors AFTER the counselors have meticulously analyzed each student's transcript and handed in their programming to meet hard and fast deadlines -- NO EXCEPTIONS.

GUIDANCE IN ROTATION

After 16 weeks in rotation at various high schools, I was appointed to fill a temporary vacancy at A. Philip Randolph Campus High School, which is on the grounds of City College (the Old Music and Art building) by David Fanning, the Principal. I started on February 11, in a marvelously collegial Guidance Department with a nurturing Principal and A. P. of Guidance.

FINAL OBSERVATION

We need a change to the field of guidance. It has to be more defined by New York State Law and Union Contract.

The basic problem is that with the current Mayor, to judge anything, you have to be able to objectively assess it by counting something. (City Hall doesn't go for the "Not everything that counts can be counted" idea or that "not everything that can be counted counts" -- which is the area where guidance counselors now reside.) To make the field more tangible, I propose the following:

1) That current counselors be paid to learn conversational Spanish at Berlitz (not at some Mickey Mouse P.D.);

2) That any counselor who would like to upgrade their computer skills be given the funds to do so at a recognized institution (not at Mickey Mouse P.D.).

3) That counselors determine what their professional development will be on professional development days. Too often Principals ignore the Union contract and ask counselors to forgo PD.

4) Counselors ought to be recognized as the authority when it comes to programming. They have to be the TOP not the down of the top down.

Further, students can be assigned to see their counselors with permanent appointments every month and assigned to one group every month. It turns the phrase "if"

I can see my counselor" to "WHEN I see my counselor...."

Should Principals wish counselors to interrupt class

lessons, the logistics of this ought to come from the

Principal with a formal memo to teachers and not left up to

counselors to be a major distraction to classroom lessons.

At the moment, Principals ignore the Union contract

with impunity. The Union has to unilaterally rectify this

and not with a million little grievance hearings that are a

waste of time and a threat to many counselors who are

reluctant to "speak up."

It's time to expunge all the ridiculous listings of the

duties of THE COUNSELOR written by the DOE and also

by APs. These listings could not be carried out if you

worked 24 hours a day and just serve to promote "guilt."

What is needed is a minute realistic analysis of the position

of counselor. A thorough assessment of what counselors

are asked to do during a school day and evaluated in terms

of how much time there is "IN REALITY." This should be step one with counselors reaching consensus and then going to Michael Mulgrew of the UFT to see how this can be effected.

Without change, all the expertise of counselors will be greeted with ... (see Opening Observation -- page 1).

About The Author

Marcia Horenstein received her Master's Degree in Guidance and Counseling from Hunter College. She went to Hunter/ Lehman College as an undergraduate majoring in English Literature, and graduating with a B.A. Phi Beta Kappa. She grew up in New York City and graduated from the High School of Performing Arts as a Drama Major Mrs. Horenstein taught English in middle and high school. She did her practicum in guidance at Murry Bergtraum in group dynamics and was hired by Bergtraum afterwards.

Made in the USA
Lexington, KY
06 October 2013